CW00835735

The First Wife's Tale

The First Wife's Tale

MERRYN WILLIAMS

Shoestring Press

Typeset and printed by Q3 Print Project Management Ltd, Loughborough, Leics
(01509) 213456

Published by Shoestring Press
19 Devonshire Avenue, Beeston, Nottingham, NG9 1BS
(0115) 925 1827
www.shoestringpress.co.uk

First published 2007
© Copyright: Merryn Williams
The moral right of the author has been asserted.
ISBN 13: 978 1 904886 46 4
ISBN 10: 1 904886 46 9

Shoestring Press gratefully acknowledges financial assistance from Arts Council England

ACKNOWLEDGEMENTS

Some of these poems have appeared in *Aesthetica, The Affectionate Punch, Aireings, Avocado, Black Mountain Review, Cadenza, Cyphers, Dreamcatcher, Envoi, Equinox, Fire, Interchange, Krax, Magma, New Welsh Review, New Writer, Obsessed with Pipework, Openings, Orbis, Other Poetry, Pennine Ink, Poetry Ireland Review, Poetry Monthly, Poetry News, Poetry Review, Poetry Scotland, Psychopoetica, Pulsar, Rain Dog, Romulus, Roundyhouse, Scintilla, Seam, Second Light, Smoke* and the website of Iraq Occupation Focus. 'Following the Coffin' won first prize and 'Survivor's Sonnet' second prize in the Ware Poets Competitions of 2001 and 2006; 'As Dictated' was the winner of the Second Light poetry competition 2003.

CONTENTS

In memory of my father-in-law
William Spooner Hemp

THE BEREAVEMENT FILES

MIDNIGHT IN AN EMPTY STUDY
for my father-in law, Professor William Spooner Hemp, F.R Ae.S.

Out of the workshop, out of the dusty 'forties
you stroll, a young man with curly tousled hair,
pipe stuck between your teeth, and drop-dead gorgeous.
You structured bridges. Kept planes in the air.

Behind you stretched a line of skilled mechanics,
coopers, the men who built the early Fords.
Photoelasticity, Aerodynamics –
incomprehensible! My tools are words,

so poor and weak. I've cleared your bookshelves, closely
shadowed by that young man I never knew.
Perhaps he'll wander in, amused to find me
at your desk, writing poems about you.

Midnight; tobacco scent rises from the furrowed
pages of your classics, Eddington and Jeans.
This gap is wider than between two cultures.
I sob, who never understood machines.

REMEMBERING TAID, IN CLEVEDON
for my father-in-law, Bill

Now you're gone, my mind goes back to that baby
I didn't know, who lived less than a day,
the child you seldom spoke of, born in wartime
at Clevedon on the Severn estuary.
A healthy boy, but shortly to be dead;
mistakes were made, the forceps crushed his head.

And now I've come to Clevedon, on this shining
March Wednesday, walked along the rundown pier.
Birds splash all day through freezing sunlit water;
light fades; a long, long time since you were here.
I've seen the hills, the estuary's faint blue,
the drab Victorian front you briefly knew.

Her labour dragged on; you were fire-watching
(those being the days when fathers weren't let in),
raced back at dawn. No doubt the gulls were shrieking
outside. (I wasn't there, I wasn't born).
The one time in your adult life, she said,
you hugged the dying child for hours and cried.

It's true. But I recall you always smiling,
the first to crack the code or get the joke,
or filling people's glasses. If I argued
you'd say, 'Go on. I'd love to see you drunk'.
I've stood here hours, birds floating far from land
and Severn shifting endless grains of sand.

Remembering, when I passed you your first grandchild
at twelve hours old (the boy who called you Taid),
you held him gingerly and said, apropos
of nothing I'd said, 'We had one who died'.
The long parade is empty; time to go.
It's dusk. And I'm the one who's weeping now.

Taid – in Welsh, grandfather.

TOTAL ECLIPSE

The moon in total eclipse
as I watch from a darkened kitchen.
The children's eyes, soon bored,
flick from the pale gold globe
again to their TV.
Look! I urge. Look at the moon!

I knew someone who crossed
my skies. He moved quite slowly.
For years I could have observed him,
but looked elsewhere. I am
no wiser than the children.
And now? The eclipse is total.

THIS IS GOING TO BE ONE OF THOSE DAYS

when I don't cry. I've had
five out of thirty-one
without any tears. Not even
that faint, annoying prick
you sense at the back of the eyes.

I'm not going to listen to Handel's
Where'er you walk, or gaze
at certain photographs,
or play that video
which is trapped, and rotates in my head.

And if I get to six
p.m., I'll pour a drink,
congratulating myself
on having come so far.
It's not quite over. In bed
I'll pick up something light
and relaxing. Another day.

COLD COMFORT

You came back one sub-zero night. Outside
the cats yowled, died and froze stiff as a board.
And Mars swung close to earth, and sheet-ice crawled
over the canal. I'd gone quite late to bed
but couldn't sleep, got up again to hear
the forecast, sloshed your whisky. Clocks chimed two.
The lights had fused. I heard your knock. The door
resisted, but I forced it open. You
stood smiling on the pavement; the cold air
swept into my house. Your hands were turning blue
and fresh snow clung all over your coat. I knew
I should be overjoyed. Why was I sure
I'd soon wake up? And why could I see no
footprints from left or right in all that snow?

THE TRAPPINGS AND THE SUITS OF WOE

Wearing black now means nothing. The Victorians
did it for every fourth cousin. But I think
this sable suit appears – just one more outfit.
(My mouth is sandpaper. My eyes are ink).
They've no idea. If it could bring you back
I'd walk round all my life in swathes of black.

OTMOOR

That's the path we took through Otmoor;
summer grasses fringe the track;
squares, mint-green, in each direction.
On my own, I'm heading back.

Lewis Carroll placed his chess match
in the 'curious country' here.
Years fly, one by one the pieces
on the chessboard disappear.

You'd be out in front, and talking
mathematics with your son.
Bored, I'd hang behind, forget you;
opportunities have gone.

So I trudge this path's cracked surface,
thinking of the words not said.
If I walked round one more corner
should I glimpse you miles ahead?

Elm trees grew here, when I came here
first. The time of elms is past.
Crickets, green-winged moths on Otmoor,
swarm like ants. Cut down like grass.

ON THE TIDELINE

Slowly, he came round.
He knew this was the Intensive Care Unit, but he'd been dreaming
of sixty years back, walking Yarmouth sands with his father,

who'd told him about Newton,
the discovery of light, how the seven colours
blend into white at last, and how he had said:

I seem to myself to have been like a boy playing
next to the sea, picking up some bright shell or pebble
while before me the mighty ocean lay unexplored.

Three doctors sat round his bed.
They introduced themselves as specialists, so he knew
this was crunch time. One said:

'Good afternoon, Mr Smith.
A scientist, aren't you? Yes, a distinguished scientist.
Four days we've been reducing your medication

so you can understand what's going on. It isn't
good news, unfortunately. If we end the treatment
now, you will die. If we continue, you will

still die, some weeks or months from now. That would mean
kidney machines, exhaustion, a long struggle
and no good outcome. What do you wish us to do?'

Next to the German Ocean, his father had told him
the shells he liked to pick up were the hard casing
of creatures that lived in the sand or rocks, whose bodies

were washed out by the sea when they died. 'There is no God' –
he thought – 'but I can cope with that'. How the old man,
a parson, had grieved when he had made the decision

to follow truth step after logical step! He said:
'I prefer to die now, when I'm in control. Please take
that oxygen mask; it will not be needed'. The February light
  dribbled away.

The grandchildren came in,
in tears, prepared to argue. The girl, in particular, looked
like him. He thought, I'll walk into the darkness

open-eyed; the colours will not be lost, the atoms
regroup themselves. 'I am leaving', he said, and turned
to the ocean.

CELEBRITY DESERT ISLAND

SURFING

Some people drop into a sly black hole.
I surf the net, find young good-looking men
I knew years back, now bald and gross, and some
others there were, I cannot find at all.

Some names are quite unusual; though I spell
them right, there's no response; they're either dead,
or stunned by beer and pills, or lost abroad;
and some I've quite forgotten. Just as well.

I count them out, those who were young with me.
There's the night sky, now slowly turning grey,
some few bright stars still burn at break of day;
behind them, multitudes that you can't see.

I type my own name in the flattened square;
eleven thousand references appear.

TROILUS ON THE SOUTH BANK

Some day I'll pass you, selling the *Big Issue*,
and though your cheeks will be reddened by cold and drink
I'll know you. But I shall pretend we're strangers,
and you'll know me, of course; I've hardly changed.
I'm not afraid of the light; I can still walk briskly,
have no deep lines. And that fur coat's brand new.
So I'll turn back, as if conscience-stricken, and hand you
a five-pound note (no gloves, I see), and the wind will
butcher the Thames, drive you under the giant concrete
pillars, and I'll say kindly, 'Keep the change'.

CELEBRITIES

Every now and then, I hear
another old friend is called Sir.

A great honour. Or I see
a face pop up on my TV

(wrinkled) that I used to know.
Another has his own chat show.

Yet another has her column,
affecting your and my opinion.

The years roll on; how they flash by
like comets in a crowded sky!

Sadly, for me it's now too late.
But I've rubbed shoulders with the great.

SHE

Malevolent, spitting poison;
old, but dressed splendidly
in a brown velvet dress and topaz fibula,
she tottered into the room, demanding homage,
just when we all thought she'd been dead for years
or at least was safely locked up in some retirement home
in Cheltenham Spa, and wouldn't be let out.
All talking stopped. We were petrified.
In a reminiscent flash
the years of her power revolved in my stunned mind.
I saw her signature, like Douglas Haig's,
on a huge heap of death warrants.
Her basilisk eyes crawled around the entire room
then fixed on me; she'd sussed what I was thinking.
'Tell me your name. I know you're not one of mine.
I'm going to exterminate you'.

IN THE BEGINNING

It had been going on for twenty years.
In the beginning, this had not been meant.
For all the doubts, the croaking classes' sneers,
and all the obvious problems, our intent
was for a short, sharp shock. When it began,
our aim was, to humiliate that man.

Our motives were the highest. We had seen
the burning villages, the refugees;
heard every night, enough to crack the screen,
those tales of sickening atrocities.
Bomb for a week, they said, *and he'll cave in*,
but not, *read history, see how wars begin.*

And now I see no way out of this mess
except – more of the same. We have to drop
yet more bombs. I'm aware they cause distress.
Alas, it's now impossible to stop.
The numbers mount. More sinned against than sinning
is what we were. At least, in the beginning.

FOUND POEM
from a headline in the *Sun*

I sat the kids down and said, look, I could lose my job
over this. I want you to understand, it's serious.
No, don't try to stop me. I've taken this decision
because, well, I think it's the right thing to do. I've thought
a lot. I am prepared to make the sacrifice.

As you know, I don't talk very much about my religion.
It's always been there and, well, it runs deep, but I
don't force it, I hope, down others' throats. I mean that
when a man – or, indeed, woman – is at a crossroads
in life, you fall back on first principles, and if
the whole world is against you, but you know,
in your heart, you're doing the right thing, that gives you
the courage to keep on.

                    I am prepared
to go so far as to say that those who are
opposed to me (as you know, there are quite a few of them!)
are, in some sense, sincere in their beliefs.
But, well, they're, simply, wrong. And all those who
aren't with me, are against me. I hope that's
quite clear. So, hey, let's go. Let's start a war.

THE SURGEON

I had the bastard on the table
for half an hour. His heart had stopped
but his brain was working, scheming
as I attended to him – my jaw dropped
when I saw who it was. I knew
if he got up and walked away
people would die. Of course, my training
took over; I pumped air into
his lungs; the thought had shocked me; I put off
that problem for another day.
Soon he bounced back, as you know;
an academic question, now.
I gave him all that I was able.
I had the bastard on the table.

THE PRISON GOVERNOR SPEAKS

They'll be after you, once they know. But you have a short start,
and then all hell will break loose; they'll all follow the blood trail,
howling and snapping, each wanting a little chunk of you.
Yes, they're despicable. Still, when all's said and done,
you brought this grief on yourself. I was not consulted.
A higher court decided. You have what you asked for,
freedom. Go, then, make whatever you can of it.
The photos are out of date; faces change in prison.
Innocent persons may be attacked, but you
have no scarlet stamp on your forehead; you look ordinary.
Only the space inside your head is different
and even I don't know what's there. I am neutral.
I wouldn't have lifted a finger to help, but now
I will do nothing to stop you, nor drop hints
to those who are on your track, and there'll be several.
The law will protect you, and if in fact it doesn't,
that was your choice, to die outside this place. Your bags
are packed, you'll be travelling light henceforth; your cell
swept clean of your dust and fingerprints, prepared for
the next celebrity occupant. Now go.

THE FIRST WIFE'S TALE, AND OTHERS

THE FIRST WIFE'S TALE

I am wiped out. They do not speak my name.
She has it all now – children, goods, the lot.
No contest; I am dead and have no claim.

She walks in – the surroundings are the same –
pours tea, snaps roses' heads. And I shall rot.
I am wiped out and they don't speak my name.

Routines go on; she drives my children home
from school and tucks the baby in his cot.
I won't protest; I'm dead and have no claim.

She entertains his friends – the ones who came
before my time – smiles, savours all she's got.
I am wiped out. They do not speak my name.

You hear faint whispers, hints she has no shame,
but it no longer matters who did what,
considering I am dead, and have no claim.

The man we loved gets very little blame;
she did, but now she's here, and I am not.
I am wiped out and they don't speak my name,
seeing that I am dead, and have no claim.

KNOCKING OVER THE KING

I resign. It's like the chess congress, in that town by the sea,
where men from a dozen time-zones
sit in deep concentration, while the quiet crowds drift past;
here's one alphabet they all comprehend.

All day I've been manoeuvring to avoid my fate,
December sunlight streams through plate-glass windows.
But it grows dark early, there's a flurry of snow
and the lamps are coming on; you've outclassed me.

The afternoon wears on and, in whispers, they discuss us;
men go out to smoke, the board-boys are flagging.
The pawns are lost, and the minor grandees;
your rooks and queen are trained on my stronghold.

You understand the patterns,
each one elegant, unique as the snowflake.
Your next move is a classic; this game will go in the books.
Time to knock over my king.

CHARLOTTE'S BABY

I dreamed my sisters came back, but they looked different,
fashionably dressed, and they were poking fun at me.
It was worse than when they died, because then I could hope
for a happy reunion. Now I have no sisters.

My window overlooks a great sea of ancient
chest-tombs, where the six of us sat in bright weather
chewing our crusts. Scarlet fever, tuberculosis
cut swathes through our parish, but I have a second chance.

I know my baby is a girl; she hasn't quickened
but I can feel her weightless skeleton, cradled in my bloodstream.
The old women say that if you are sick repeatedly
(as I have been this week) it's a girl, and healthy.

I'll name her Emily, Anne, Maria, Elizabeth;
we'll read and sew by firelight; I'll talk French to her.
I scarcely remember those years of producing books
instead of children. This is a new chapter.

Today I walked as far as the waterfall, swollen
with melted snow, raging in winter power,
and light sprang out, though it was wild and cloudy,
in flashes, as on that day we saw three suns.

I want her to live; I know I shall be glad when the nausea
recedes. My clothes are drenched, but the heavy rain
has cleared and left the western sky faint yellow
like a starved crocus, forcing its way through the last snow.

THE GARDENER'S WIFE

I told my husband, get the cart out;
I think I know where the missing child is.
But they won't find him alive, after all this time.

We'd wondered, through four weeks' high summer;
poppies, nasturtiums wilted; stag beetles and horseflies
buzzed all day, in the intolerable sun.

His father had only stopped at the inn briefly
in fading August light. They raised the alarm within minutes.
How could one small boy have slipped through so many hands?

It wasn't the twenty pounds reward I cared for.
I only thought he might not have gone down, but upwards,
past the deep little llyn, and if he saw Brecon's lights

far below, they would only disorient him further.
It was a Sunday. I said, let's get the cart out;
the dream told me to make for the high ground.

*The memorial to Tommy Jones is on Craig Cwm Llwych in the
Brecon Beacons.*

A SISTER RECALLS

My brother had a quiet voice; men used to strain
to hear him from the back of a crowded room.

My brother spoke in the debate on conscription, said
he'd always be last to go forth and the first to retreat.

When the newspapers cried, 'Young men, march forward!'
he sat in one place and smiled, 'I'm a coward'.

He liked chess problems, hiking above the snow;
should have been a girl because girls didn't go.

My brother was lost in the summer advance;
his name is written on blue glass

in the college chapel. They dedicated
the window before the Lord Lieutenant

and other dignitaries, swathed in black.
I went there and looked once. I shan't go back.

NO NAMES

It's midnight, in a town I never saw.
You are asleep. I'm not, but reading late,
a hundred miles further south. And years have passed
since we last spoke. I caused you so much pain
you'd like to blank me out. And certainly,
we're not, at this moment, thinking of one another.
But sometimes, I stalk in and out of your imagination,
as you of mine. Your child is sleeping soundly,
sucking her furry giraffe. In your bad dream,
you turn, unconsciously reach for your wife's pillow.
You think she's at her creative writing class.
Actually she's with her lover. As the clocks change
he moans, 'Must you go?' Dark, fire and water turning
to cutting hail. While in some third dimension,
though we don't want to remember, you and I
walk arm in arm through magic, bulldozed streets –
it happened, can't be totally denied.
I close my book. She garages the car,
creeps in, finds her half of the bed is cold,
and hears your breathing, thinks, 'he'll never know ....'

SATURDAY NIGHT OUT

Sometimes, working late, with books and notepaper
littering my desk, I thought the building felt
unnaturally quiet. Then I remembered it was
Saturday night, and, this being a women's college,
they were all out. Or sat in dark rooms, pretending
that they were out. Only my lamp burned on
regardless. Around twelve, in deep exhaustion,
and as the parties reached their climax, I
fell into bed. Later they'd come on tiptoe
down passages, doors would cautiously close. My friend
was out all night with that eligible young man
who died at twenty-seven.

AFTERTASTE

The orange taste of cointreau, and the rich
smooth taste of maraschino chocolate, plus
the bitter taste of that especially
imported sherry, still remain with me.

The wet cold streets of that abandoned town
where rubbish spills from skips; I'm there alone,
wake with dry mouth, remembering all it cost
to walk the other way, refuse your kiss.

FOLLOWING THE COFFIN
'How is your life with the other one?'
                    Marina Tsvetayeva

I am following you, down the disused corpse-road,
on the edge of a crowd of strangers.
Four strong men carry you, you who were weak,
and a hard frost is cracking the stones.

Orion is rising, and here's a full moon.
A murmur of north-country voices.
Dogs howl from the farms, all the faces look stressed.
On Helm Crag, the last of the snow.

So I follow you, as I once watched your career
at a distance. Your wife and your friend
are in the crowd, practically touching.
She doesn't know I'm here.

I've got a new name that disguises my past,
and the darkness covers plenty.
Did you like what you got? It was she, at the end,
not I, who slid the knife in.

Yes, my interest in you never died, though you did.
I know where the bodies are buried,
and walk close to her, under that changeable moon,
each following your coffin.

SURVIVOR'S SONNET

Like Anna Karenina, I loved two men
with the same name. And one of them was good
in every way, no sickness was in him;
the other was a virus in my blood.
One built me up, the other pulled me down;
comfort – despair – bread – stones – one dark, one light.
I gripped the lifebelt, hoping not to drown
but almost did. The train rushed through the night,
a hundred miles an hour, out of control,
smashed any small scared creature in its way;
hooters wailed through the dark hours, until all
came round, rubbed eyes, unclean at break of day.
The great wheels slowed and stalled; I saw again
the man who stopped me falling off the train.

MOONLIGHT

In the small hours, when the moon
casts sheets of light across our bed,
I start up. *Where are my children?*
Wandering about the world,
not thinking much of home. I stare
at their photographs, in dusty
moonlight, wish them here.

In another house, two children
(I love them, but their genes aren't mine)
wake up, sweating. *Where's my father?*
Gradually, they will remember.
He's only ten miles down the road,
moon glistening on a field of stone,
and they can go there, any time.

WHITBY NIGHTS

When a lonely photographer,
one hundred years ago, in Whitby,
went out to investigate
pitch dark, swaying lamps, the sea –
white horses in a frenzy –

He'd have walked, wrapped in oilskins,
to the extreme end of the jetty,
rigged up his antique camera
undistracted by the human;
who would come in winter?

The prints are treasured. You can enter
a present-day shop, and buy one
at a price. He didn't often
point his camera at people –
like me, he didn't like them.

All in this town has changed, except
the sea. A stray Victorian
might know his way, though, in the small hours.
He and I have walked these streets,
but not in the same time-frame.

OVERHEARD IN THE CANCER WARD

Here's the divorce paper. Best that you should sign it.
(It's up to you, of course). I'll guide your hand.
Then I can be with her, and we can form a
new family. I knew you'd understand.

No, I've not brought Jamie, don't want to upset him;
he's with her now. You know you can't get dressed.
Lie back and look at the grey sky through the windows.
It's done. I told you it was for the best.

You were so pretty when I first saw you;
when you look in the hand mirror now, remember this.
Well, got to go. Keep the ring. I'll tell Jamie
you're fine. That you send him a big kiss.

THE PHILOSOPHER'S STONE

People must have asked this question:
'Why do you devote your life
to something which is not going to
give you a successful outcome?
You, an intelligent man!'

'Because I wish, like Roger Bacon,
to toil, while glass is blocked by snow,
not hear the traffic buzz below.
The atmosphere is cold and clear
at the top of my high tower.

'Lights spring on in my computer;
the database is vast, reveals
new leads, a chance to manufacture
the longed-for gold dust. I'll go on
chasing the philosopher's stone'.

Silence, as in a cathedral;
last week's work is thrown out,
the atoms bunch to form a crystal,
something moves. 'You're mad'. 'Perhaps;
that is what you must accept'.

THE BOOK

He made that marvellous beginning;
the book was solid, bound in green –
footnotes, sources, all impressive,
stacked up: the classic text.
The best mind of his generation,
some said – but there was more to write,
there always is. And then they wondered,
What will he do next?

The years passed; nothing happened. If they
asked, some winter night, *Where is he?*
the answer was a shrug.
'At some meeting, selling papers
on the corner of a street'.
The moon appears through cloud, goes out.
Others passed him, had a line
of books stamped with their name.

See the folly. That career
which blazed so brilliantly, gone;
it won't recover. And he's ageing,
walked straight into a blind alley
chosen by himself.
He looked unperturbed, said only,
'Does it matter, if there aren't
more books upon the shelf?'

BLOOD DONOR

It all floats back. I'm staring at the ceiling,
as others queue, to give blood for Vietnam;
tense as a cat, and carefully ignoring
the crimson trickle leaking from my arm.
I see you stand up, much taller than the others,
stagger, somebody guides you to a bed;
stare through the crowd, my interest never wavers,
focussed on you – but *touch me not*, you'd said.
The capsule cracks; high windows, August heat,
me lying on the white unspotted sheet.

There's no real sequel. All those students scattered,
some dead. Vietnam stopped bleeding long ago.
I turn the page; my son becomes an adult,
walks those same streets, the age and height of you.
In dreams, I feel the needle scratch my wrist,
and think of blood, our blood that never mixed.

VIRTUAL OBITUARY

DIED, in his ninety-fourth year, 4th of May
1869, THOMAS LANGLOIS LEFROY,
Lord Chief Justice of Ireland, Member of Parliament
for Dublin University, Baron of
the Irish Court of Exchequer.

BORN, 8th of January 1776.
Trinity College, Dublin. Won many prizes.
Called to the Bar. K.C.

Of Huguenot stock, he was a typical
Protestant Tory; despite his age, took part in
the trials of '48.

MARRIED, first, 1797, JANE,
the daughter of the Reverend George AUSTEN
of Steventon, county of Hampshire, by which lady
(who died 1798) he had issue
a stillborn son. And second ....

THE EVIL EYE

The force of malevolence is strong. I never
believed she could harm me, but when her evil eye
was trained in my direction, I began
to fall apart.

She'd swim into view, that yellow
single orb seeming to burn me up; her silent
loathing communicated itself to others. I said,
ignore her, she's got no real power. It's superstition.

The cat died. That was not much, but then I was never
quite well, and there were other things, small pieces of bad luck.
My few friends backed off; none wanted to offend her
and people avoided stepping in my shadow.

And then, well, it was terrifying. I heard them
night after night, a witches' coven, dancing on my roof.
Hard as November hail and in a full unblinking moon, they
proclaimed, I wasn't wanted. Here or anywhere.

I am covered in blotches and weeping sores; I creep out
late, when there's no one about, all strip me naked with their looks.
Wherever I go, she'll still be there; a hundred eyes now watch me.
I know it's her doing but people think I'm mad.

THE WRONG MAN

There's a crude electric bulb, and the room looks naked,
carpetless, too small. If your mother could see you now!
What are you doing with this man? you'll inquire
later – much later. Now you aren't thinking straight.

You loved and admired a man quite unlike this one
some time ago; since then, you've lowered your sights.
And that man now groping you isn't the right man
(as you knew, in fact, all this time).

He's out there in the dark, unhappy as you are,
perhaps trying to talk, deeply bored, to some girl;
or at this precise moment at work on a chess problem,
studying Einstein.

And you don't know his name yet. Two halves of a perfect
whole don't come together but free-float, unmatched.
For now, there is only this room with cheap furniture,
where too many have come and gone.

NOT THE ETERNAL TRIANGLE

I knew that man was a threat.
The triangle, me and you
and him. The first time we met –

a college garden; blue
lilies; odd-scented, rare
carnations. I don't forget.

Falling in love, but I feared –
what? I didn't know.
That man with the black beard
who ought not to have been there.

Half a lifetime ago.

I sit at my desk and see
August sunlit air,
petals dropping like snow,
a false acacia tree;
and nothing as it appeared,
him and you and me.

DEEP WATER

Had it been up to me, I'd have let *Bluebird*
stay in the deep cold waters of Coniston,
and never gaped, voyeurist, as the dredgers
raised that bright paint again into the sun.

And all those murdered women, under cover
of darkness, thrust in this and other lakes –
what good to stage a pseudo-resurrection,
draping their bones in coffins, flowers, flags?

Skiddaw, Scafell, the Old Man calmly circle
the waters; colours of the trees and sky
spread wide; the stone you drop disturbs the surface
and sinks; I think it's no bad place to lie.

THE CRAMPED ROOMS
remembering Anne Frank

We lived on top of one another;
my wife, the children and the rest.
In those cramped rooms, tempers clashed,
vicious rows, queues for the bathroom.
I taught the two girls French and German.

But when we're out of here, I said,
I'll travel. So I watched the skies,
envied the birds their short, hard lives.
Now – I thought *– all depends on me,*
but they'll grow up. And I'll be free.

And now I am. I walk the pavements,
step on to a boat, a plane,
broadcast, lift my hat to strangers.
The world is wide. I'd give it all
to live in those cramped rooms again.

FANNY BRAWNE

So here I am, walking through the Boboli gardens
decorously with my children, who aren't his,
who run in late spring sunlight, so much warmer
than in England. They make me look my age.

Their faces radiant and they don't glance backwards,
bunches of crimson anemones in their hands.
He said it was the blood of the god Adonis
which fell in bright slow drops, spotting the woods.

One day I might go south to Rome, and sit on
the quiet grass of the English cemetery.
His name is *writ in water*. I've told my husband
nothing. It feels like adultery.

I know the place only from descriptions
by poets; wandering flocks of sheep and goats
chew on the daisies, and the youthful shepherds
doze briefly near his stone on summer nights.

That's a good dream, but I won't return to Hampstead
and its chill winds. The wild boar gashed his thigh.
His sister never forgave me for getting married
and I think his friends hated me. When I die

they'll put me far from where he is;
angels and broken lyres will crowd around
my headstone – *Frances, wife of Louis Lindon* –
and vicious words won't gore us, underground.

AFTER MANDELSTAM

Sleepless, I turn to Homer. Wind in sails.
I have read half the Catalogue of Ships –
that line – enormous, unmistakable
as cranes in flight – that once loomed over Greece.

A wedge of cranes that points to distant lands.
Foam on the old kings' beards. Where are you going?
The book drops to the floor. And what would Troy
mean to you, old Achaeans, but for Helen?

The sea and Homer – all is moved by love.
Which should I listen to? Homer is dead.
And the dark ocean booms – rhetorical,
crashing, tremendous, behind my pillowed head.

PILTDOWN

I am turning over the bones; I claw my way back to where it began.
Sussex, a gravel pit, speedwell blooming on the Long Man.

Mastodons hump through my dreams, thick furs in the fearful cold.
Yes, it's a bitter day, but I feel less keenly now I am old.

Forty years ago, glory days, before brains began to grow dull.
As you say, I'm in the famous painting, measuring the skull.

All the rest of the group are gone. That man was a fraud, a thief,
but even learned men believe what they want to believe.

The Natural History Museum closes its gates, there's a spreading shame.
None escape; like the bones, each distinguished reputation stained.

Piltdown Man glares up from my book, ape jaw and ferocious grin.
I think you are probably right. But it will take some time to sink in.

BELIEVE IT

A mystery. His car still parked
in the usual place; his coat
draped on the back of his chair.
CCTV picked him up
walking out of the building.
His credit cards, all there.

But there is a web of canals
in the city. A man could go
out at that hour of the day
and not be missed. I know
his colleagues, his family can't
believe it.

The mind has its own mesh
of deep canals. Things lie
for years in the one place.
Push your card in that hole
in the wall, and get no response.
Believe it.

AS THE VETERAN TOLD ME .....

Knowing the military police
were after him, he stayed
long hours inside a cinema,
watching the troops parade
again, again across the screen
and then 'over the top'.
No use, when he at last got home
they'd come to pick him up.

Or you could sit inside the Tube
and feel it roll and roll,
and count the stops, and think you're safe
from every breathing soul.
At 1 a.m. it shuts; the street
is full of bad night air;
the faceless men you fear to meet
already may be there.

I have this dream: the squares are dark,
I used to know this place.
I loiter, take the long road round,
not one familiar face.
The Circle Line is closed; I shun
the men I cannot see.
No use; when I at last get home
they're here, to handcuff me.

ADMIRING THE STILL LIVES

Light-headed, I walk through the spaces of the gallery –
(they back away, don't like me). All those gold-
encrusted virgins and landscapes hang unimportant,
in one dimension. I smell only the food.

Brown loaves. Cool wine in the glittering decanter.
Redcurrants. Water melon, deep pure green.
Fish on its silver salver, a knife ready
to cut it. Only this field of air between.

The juices rise in my gorge; I'd like to
snatch, rip the canvas open. It's a day
and night since I've eaten. And the well-fed thousands
stare blind, float past me in the gallery.

THE ENGLISH DISEASE

Twenty years I knew him,
never said a word
in all our many meetings
his wife could not have heard.

Talked about the weather
(the English never change),
work, of course, the Test Match;
he noticed nothing strange.

Much the same as usual
my life is chugging on.
Twenty years I knew him,
another ten have gone.

But, waking in the small hours,
I sicken, all the same,
to see those lovely features
in the crematorial flame.

HE REVISITS EARTH

I landed feet first, in a rush of wind.
Grey-silver light; I saw the rarest owl
sail past; time was when I'd have noted that.
There's dust on my binoculars. And all

seems much the same. She's sitting in my chair,
red-eyed, and some years older. But the gate
hangs loosely, not the way I liked. I can't
unlock this window. Bring me up to date.

Where are the children? No response; the house
is firmly barred; they've left me far behind.
I stand here shivering; February stars
chill to the bare bone. Who has seen the wind?

ROOTS

ANCESTRESS

Margaret Williams, my great-grandmother,
knew little but hard labour.

I have a photograph of her,
taken during the Great War,

one son at the front. She looks
much older than she really was;

a labourer's wife in stiff black dress,
face deeply lined, dead in her forties.

Drawing well-water, cropping stones,
she knew none of today's machines

except the camera. There exists
another photograph, in which

she looks directly at me, laughing.
I hope life gave her something.

NAMESAKE
for my husband John Hemp

I see your great-great-grandfather. He's walking
down some pale-grey street in Victorian Yarmouth
to register the birth of his son Thomas,
his only mark on history, that I know.
It's 1848; the Chartists massing
on Gloucester Green, and Dickens is in Yarmouth –
'The town and tide mixed up like toast and water' –
and boats go down, and undersized thin figures
loom up, and then are gone, through wraiths of mist.
I can't quite fix his features, as the window
fogs over when I breathe on it. He's kindly,
good with his hands, a young man by our standards.
I watch; he goes into the office, puts down
his bag of tools and signs your name *John Hemp*.
He doesn't know me, but I know his history;
born in the workhouse, never saw his father –
whose bones lie far from Norfolk, who was lost
that time the press-gang snatched him for Napoleon's
last war. A family of cousins died
in Smallburgh Hundred House. He says some words
I miss, hands back the scratchy antique pen.
This is a man who slips through lists and records.
I've not yet pinned him down. There is a cold wind, and
room and street vanish.

John Hemp was born in Smallburgh workhouse on or around 18th
March 1813. His mother always claimed that her 'husband' had
been taken away by the press-gang and never returned from the
Napoleonic wars.

MARY ANN
Mary Ann George married Thomas Hemp on 19th August 1873

Did she think
as she signed
that she was signing her death warrant;
that the baby now leaping
beneath her best dress
would be first of ten;
that the two-year-old, Tommy,
would cough out his life
as she helplessly held him,
November in Yarmouth, thick fog
round the two-up two-down
near the quay;
that the virile young man at her side
would go on to marry
another woman, outlive her by three decades?
No, she was happy,
a girl who had no known father,
welcomed that day into her husband's family;
August, uncountable motes of dust
in England's largest parish church;
there was a small celebration, and she had her time in the sun.
But her son, an old man with watery eyes,
would repeat the story:
The doctor never came; father said to his face he killed her.
She was thirty-eight. It was after the last baby.

Her name
was lost, until I discovered it. When I gave birth to
her great-great-grandchild, when my temperature shot up, when
    they brought me
penicillin at dead of night, I sensed
another figure behind the nurse. It was gone by morning.
Into the dark again, treading the bloody prints of
my silent predecessor, along the shortest
and most dangerous journey. Be there when I pass, Mary Ann.

LAURA'S SONG
Laura Hemp was married on 3rd April 1899

My mother will not be there as I walk through the churchyard
my family walk with me smiling   celandines spring
in the new grass   around the illegible tombstones
no stone is on her grave   it's a bright April day.

I can do no more for the children; my father has another
wife now;   I can lay that burden down.
Seven years I looked after them. All are well, except one
who never will be. My bridegroom is waiting in the church.

On the same day that they buried my mother, a drowned man
washed up by the North Sea was laid in the next plot;
his name was never found.   Like my grandparents and parents
I pass under this porch   my name too will be lost

I shall live to see the bombing of Yarmouth; this church will
fall and be rebuilt, the glass melt in great fires.
The Norfolk accent will die on the lips of my children
they scatter   today the force passes through me.

AS DICTATED
Eliza Hemp died in spring 1892 aged about 35

I don't trust him. I don't believe he will look after my children.
He's crying, of course – tears were always easy for him.
How I fear that Barnardo's is waiting.
How I dread them being shipped to Australia.

A cluster of little heads round the big double bed; I count them.
William, Catherine, Eliza, Benjamin, Alice.
Ten, eight, six, three, one. Who is going to look after them?
And there's shouting down there in the street; we have no friends.
Do I want some better-off woman to take my baby,
give her a new name, tell her nothing about me?
Do I want my son taken into the army? –
they're on the lookout for boys. And the migrant ships
are waiting; the white race is poised to conquer the world.

And it's a grey morning
in 1892. The recording angel
is writing my name; I see him. And in this dream
I see bits of the future; my daughter going for a servant,
no man will ever marry her, and she'll die young.
Three-year-old Ben with his baby cheeks; that cough
frightens me, but I can't lift my head; I am drowning slowly
and they're clinging hard to their father. I don't trust him.

REMEMBRANCE DAY
i.m. Gabriel Hemp

My cousin Gabriel lies in the Reichswald Forest
east of the old border and deep within Germany;
my cousin old enough to have been my father
has lain since 1945 and he left no children.

Twenty years he had. There were a mother and a sister;
the line became extinct that crossed the German Ocean
centuries before; men of the same name fought against him,
no angel with a fiery sword to guard you, Gabriel.

None will ever come out of this forest; so thickly
twine the fir boughs, almost all light is excluded,
such flowers as grow are purple-pale, self-seeding;
I count the seven thousand stones and get no closer, Gabriel.

TRANSLATIONS FROM MIGUEL HERNANDEZ

BLOODY FATE

I come, like blood on blood,
like wave on wave of sea.
My soul is poppy red,
my luckless destiny
to fall on horns of fate
like the poppy.

A creature has to grow
where creatures there were none,
and more than one comes through
beneath a wrathful star,
a bad, a troubled moon.

A bloody footstep fell
across my open wound,
a planet's yellow ball,
a red and angry cloud.
I struggled into life,
they fed me bitter milk;
the first thing that I saw
on birthing, was a knife,
and wasn't that bad luck?

A red that foams. I came
along a tide of blood.
Before I had a name
my mother pushed me out,
into this greedy land
and nearer to the grave.

The anguish of the plough
has chained me to the earth;
the tools have dragged me down
and slashed me since my birth.
The scaffolding of bone,
the bougainvillea tree
of blood in every vein
roars in me.

LIKE THE BULL

Like the bull, I was born for pain
and sadness, like the bull I bear a brand
with a cruel iron thrust in my side,
and – being male – in the fruit of my groin.

Like the bull, my oversized heart
finds everything else too small.
I'm in love with a face, with a kiss – that's all –
and, like the bull, am constrained to fight.

Like the bull, I am swollen, punch-drunk,
my tongue drenched in arterial blood,
my neck is padlocked by a roaring gale.

Like the bull I go forward and back,
you torment me with your sword,
like the baited bull, like the bull